KU-622-862

HEINEMANN
Profiles

George Lucas

An Unauthorized Biography

Janet Riehecky

www.heinemann.co.uk
Visit our website to find out more information about **Heinemann Library** books.

To order:
☎ Phone 44 (0) 1865 888066
▤ Send a fax to 44 (0) 1865 314091
▢ Visit the Heinemann Bookshop at www.heinemann.co.uk to browse our catalogue
and order online.

First published in Great Britain by Heinemann Library, Halley Court, Jordan Hill, Oxford
OX2 8EJ, a division of Reed Educational and Professional Publishing Ltd.
Heinemann is a registered trademark of Reed Educational & Professional Publishing Limited.

OXFORD MELBOURNE AUCKLAND JOHANNESBURG BLANTYRE GABORONE IBADAN
PORTSMOUTH NH (USA) CHICAGO

Produced for Heinemann Library by Discovery Books Limited
Edited by Patience Coster
Designed by Ian Winton
Originated by Dot Gradations
Printed and bound in Hong Kong/China

ISBN 0 431 08643 5 (hardback)
05 04 03 02 01
10 9 8 7 6 5 4 3 2 1

British Library Cataloguing in Publication Data

Riehecky, Janet
George Lucas. – (Heinemann Profiles)
1. Lucas, George – Juvenile literature 2. Motion picture
   producers and directors – United States – Biography –
   Juvenile literature
I. Title
791.4'3'0233'092

Acknowledgements
The Publishers would like to thank the following for permission to reproduce photographs:
Bettman/Corbis pp8, 9, 24, 38; Corbis pp13, 19 (Robert Holmes), 26 (Catherine Karnow), 28, 31, 34 (Lynn
Goldsmith), 47 (Roger Ressmeyer), panel photo (Kurt Krieger); London Features International p15;
McHenry Museum, Modesto, CA pp6, 11; Popperfoto/Reuter pp17, 40, 42, 49, 51; Reuters NewMedia
Inc/Corbis pp33, 37; Rex Features pp5, 22, 44; Ronald Grant Archive pp20, 23.

Cover photograph reproduced with permission of London Features International Ltd

Every effort has been made to contact copyright holders of any material reproduced in this book. Any
omissions will be rectified in subsequent printings if notice is given to the Publisher.

Any words appearing in the text in bold, **like this**, are explained in the Glossary.

CONTENTS

WHO IS GEORGE LUCAS?

The Hollywood film industry exerts an enormous influence on our lives. Images from Hollywood movies may affect what we choose to wear, how we behave, even what we think. Ironically, one of the most powerful men in the American film business today is a shy, creative individual who tends to avoid the glitz and glamour we usually associate with Hollywood.

George Lucas has written, produced and directed some of the most successful movies ever made. During the 1970s, he entered a movie-making world dominated by older men and turned that world upside down. In his famous movie *Star Wars*, he pioneered sweeping technological changes and amazing special effects. Even more importantly, he changed the subject matter of movies and the way in which stories were told. Instead of making films about 'real-life' issues, Lucas' three *Star Wars* films were fairy-tale fantasies with non-stop action, and a mythic clash of good versus evil, with good winning through.

'Working hard is very important. You're not going to get anywhere without working extremely hard. No matter how easy it looks on the outside, it's a very, very difficult struggle.'

George Lucas

Studio executives couldn't figure out why everyone wanted to see the films – but they did. With the billions of dollars earned by the *Star Wars* and *Indiana Jones* films, Lucas has created a huge movie-making empire and changed the history of cinema itself. His movies are more watched than any others, and their influence extends around the world.

Film producer and director George Lucas.

A Strong-Willed Child

George Lucas was born on 14 May 1944. His parents, George and Dorothy Lucas, already had two daughters and so were very pleased to have a son. They named him George Walton Lucas Jnr and, almost from the minute he was born, George Snr began making plans for his son's future.

George Snr owned a **stationer's** shop in Modesto, a small town in northern California. The previous owner had regarded George Snr almost as a son, and arranged for him to take over the business when he

A 1950s' photo of the main street in Modesto.

retired. George Snr dreamed of doing the same with his own son. But George Jnr had other ideas.

George Jnr was small, but what he lacked in height, he made up for in stubborn determination to do things his own way. When he was just 2 $\frac{1}{2}$, he watched while some workmen tore down a wall. He proceeded to get his own hammer and chisel and went to work on another wall. Unfortunately, the wall he set to work on was not supposed to be removed!

'When kids come to me and say, "Well, how do you get into the business?" I say, "You just start doing it."'

George Lucas

George loved working with his hands. He built dolls' houses for his sisters and their friends. He made chess sets and toy cars. Once he even constructed a kid-sized rollercoaster in his back garden. He started a neighbourhood newspaper and made his first film – a **stop-motion** sequence of plates stacking and unstacking themselves – before he was twelve. And he demonstrated not only creative talent, but also a good business sense. When he and a friend turned a garage into a haunted house, he charged admission. Children lined up around the **block** (as they would one day line up to see his films) waiting to get in.

A MIND OF HIS OWN

Lucas says that he enjoyed his childhood, but he also recalls feeling uncertain and depressed much of the time. Some of these feeling may be attributed to his relationship with his parents.

His mother had always been frail, and the birth of George's younger sister, Wendy, drained Dorothy's strength. During George's childhood, she was always in poor health and frequently in hospital. She

adored 'Georgie', but left most of his care to their housekeeper, Mildred 'Till' Shelley.

George Snr was another matter. He was a stern **Methodist** who believed in the value of hard work. He put in long hours at his store and expected the same kind of effort from his son. When George was eleven, his father insisted that he mow the lawn with a push-mower. This was very difficult for George physically. He was short and thin. So he worked out a plan. For weeks he saved his pocket money. When he had $35, he borrowed $25 more from his mother. Then he went out and bought a power mower. George Snr couldn't decide whether to be angry with his son for avoiding the lesson he wanted to teach him, or proud of his resourcefulness.

George often demonstrated the persistence and **tenacity** his father expected of him, but only when working on projects of his own choosing. This caused tension in the family because his early passions were comic books, television, and rock and roll music – not his father's store.

Rock and roll artist Elvis Presley was an inspiration for many 1950s' teenagers.

'There were three or four teachers along the way that inspired me. I wasn't particularly good in English – I didn't really like it that much – but I had a high school English teacher who was just brilliant. I don't know whether he taught me very much, but he certainly inspired me to be creative and try to write things.'
George Lucas

School bored George and his grades reflected his boredom. He said later, 'I always wanted to learn something other than what I was being taught… I wanted to enjoy school in the worst way and I never could. I think it's a waste of time to spend a lot of energy trying to beat education into somebody's head. They're never going to get it unless they want to get it.'

His one interest in school was art. He enjoyed creating pictures and even made his own greetings cards, but here again he wanted to follow his own ideas. In those days, such creativity was not encouraged. His art teacher scolded him for drawing his own pictures instead of doing the assignment.

THE TEENAGE REBEL

Things became worse as George entered his teenage years. When he was fifteen, his father purchased land outside of town and moved the family there. George was now cut off from his friends. He began retreating to his room and his collection of comic books and rock and roll records whenever he was home, emerging only to eat or watch television.

His father tried to encourage his former interest in building things by providing a place to work and new materials. He even bought his son a 35mm camera and turned a bathroom into a **darkroom** for him. George wasn't interested. But eventually a new obsession coaxed him out of his room: cars.

Cars, especially racing cars, became a passion to outshine anything else in his life. George begged and pleaded and finally got his parents to buy him a car. In his mind it was barely a car: it was a Fiat Bianchina, with just a two-cylinder engine. But it provided him with an escape. He joined the other teens in Modesto, and together they **cruised** the downtown area from four in the afternoon until after midnight every Saturday night.

Downey High School, Modesto, where George was a student.

CRUISING

Cruising was a way of life for California teenagers in the late fifties and early sixties. During the week, kids worked on their cars, souping up engines and lowering roofs and bodies. The ideal **hot-rod** had a roof as close to the bonnet as the owner could get it; the body of the car was a few centimetres from the ground.

Cruising in downtown Modesto involved a circuit through 10th and 11th streets. These were one-way streets, going in opposite directions. Drivers cruised down 10th, turned and drove past a **block** of houses, headed back up 11th, skipped back, and began the circuit all over again. Conversations were shouted from one vehicle to another as boys tried to pick up girls. Drivers challenged one another to **drag races** at dawn, held outside of town on the

Terry the Toad

American Graffiti tells the story of four young men, on a single night of cruising. Lucas put part of himself into each character, but the one that was most like him was Terry the Toad. Like Terry, Lucas was small and socially awkward. But none of that mattered once he was behind the wheel of his hot-rod.

American Graffiti **shows the 1950s' teenage pastime of meeting up at diners and drive-in movie shows.** long, flat, country roads. Rock and roll music blared from every radio. This ritual was immortalized by Lucas in his 1973 film about youth, *American Graffiti*.

Lucas' father didn't understand any of this. He insisted that his son work at the **stationer's** to pay off the car. Lucas was supposed to make deliveries, move stock, clean the toilets, sweep the shop, and lock up when he had finished. None of this interested George Jnr. After just a few weeks, he and his father had a terrible fight, and George Snr fired him.

Family friction

When Lucas was called into Traffic Court because of his numerous traffic tickets, his father became even more certain that his son would never amount to anything.

> 'Everybody has talent, it's just a matter of moving around until you've discovered what it is.'
>
> George Lucas

Shortly after getting his driver's licence, Lucas crashed his Fiat rounding a bend at 112 kph. He wasn't badly hurt, but the car was a wreck. As he would do many times in his life, he turned seeming disaster to his advantage. He and a friend rebuilt the car, removing the crumpled roof and putting in a roll bar, souping up the engine, improving the shock absorbers, and adding professional seatbelts. If it wasn't the car of his dreams, at least it was now a genuine **hot-rod**.

Lucas became a part of the northern California racing circuit. He was becoming a talented mechanic and made friends with many of the racing car drivers. He even became the editor of a sports car club newsletter. He loved the thrill of high speeds and the challenge of winning. This was the world he wanted to be a part of.

At home, however, things still weren't good. Lucas' father was pressuring him to join the family business after he graduated from high school – *if* he graduated from high school. A week before graduation, Lucas had a 'D' average, and had not completed three courses. He and his father fought again. Lucas remembers shouting, 'There are two things I know for sure. One is that I will end up doing something with cars… and two, that I will never be president of a company.'

He was still not sure what he was going to do with his life when, on 12 June 1962, he headed to the library to study. But that trip would help him to decide his future.

Grand Prix racer

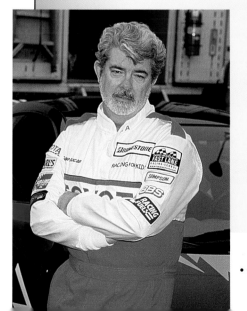

Lucas had a chance to return to his racing obsession in April 2000. He was one of fifteen celebrity drivers to compete in the pro-celebrity race at the 24th annual Toyota Grand Prix of Long Beach. Though he finished in sixteenth place, his time on the ten-lap race was only 1.04 minutes slower than that of the first place winner, Josh Brolin. Proceeds from the charity race benefited children's hospitals in southern California.

You Can't Stay 17 For Ever

On that day, Lucas spent a couple of hours at the library and then headed home, driving fast. He didn't see the Chevy Impala overtaking him. As he made a left turn, the Impala struck his car on the driver's side. Lucas' car bounced and flipped over three times. On the third roll, his seatbelt broke and he was thrown from the vehicle. The car flipped over again and slammed into a tree, still travelling at about 100 kph Lucas landed on his chest, unconscious but alive.

A miraculous escape

A neighbour saw the accident and called for help. Lucas was rushed to hospital. He had suffered two fractures, but the worst injury was to his lungs, which were **haemorrhaging**. Still, it was a miracle he hadn't been killed. Lucas thought about this, as he spent most of the summer recovering in bed.

College

Lucas began to search for a purpose to his life. His high school diploma was delivered to him in hospital, even though he hadn't finished those three courses. But his grades weren't good enough to get him into a four-year college. He thought things over and enrolled at Modesto Junior College to study sociology, anthropology, and art history.

Although he no longer dreamed of becoming a racing car driver, he still hung around race tracks with the friends he'd made on the race circuit. This time, though, he carried an 8mm movie camera that his father had given him. He became fascinated with the images he could capture on film. A friend talked him into applying to the University of Southern California (USC). To his – and his father's – amazement, he was accepted.

On the racing circuit, Lucas met Haskell Wexler, a professional cameraman in the film industry. He was filming a documentary and Lucas became his assistant. Wexler liked Lucas and encouraged him to study film at USC. He even called one of the faculty members there and told him to keep an eye on the kid. So, in the autumn of 1964, George Lucas entered USC as a film student.

Cinematographer Haskell Wexler, pictured here with actress Mary Elizabeth Mastrantonio in 1999.

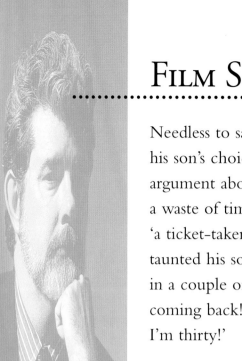

Film School

Needless to say, Lucas' father was not happy about his son's choice of subject. They had a huge argument about it. His father was certain that it was a waste of time and that Lucas would end up as 'a ticket-taker at Disneyland'. When George Snr taunted his son that he would be back in Modesto in a couple of years, Lucas shouted, 'I'm never coming back! I'm going to be a millionaire before I'm thirty!'

When it was clear that Lucas couldn't be talked out of his decision, he and his father reached an unusual compromise to cover the costs (in the United States, students have to 'pay their way' through college). George Snr 'hired' his son to go to college. Lucas' father paid the tuition and fees and gave Lucas a 'salary' of $200 a month. If Lucas didn't do well, he would be 'fired'.

'When I look back on it now, if I'd gone to art school, or stayed in anthropology, I probably would have ended up back in film. No matter which route I would have taken, I'm almost positive I would have ended up eventually in film.'

George Lucas

Feeling at home

However, at USC Lucas quickly learned that he had found his calling. He loved the entire process

of capturing an idea on film, and he loved the atmosphere and **camaraderie** of the school itself.

In those days, no one expected that a student would get a job in the film industry after graduation. The film industry did not offer such opportunities to younger people.

The University of Southern California, where Lucas studied film. Apart from actors, there were very few people under the age of fifty working at any major studio. To get into films, you had to have a personal connection to some Hollywood insider or become a **union** member. The unions issued long lists of requirements that few people could meet and they insisted on **apprenticeships** of three to five years. Instead of becoming part of the Hollywood system, George Lucas' class at college expected to make little **documentaries** outside Hollywood or to work in commercials.

> '[At USC] …my whole life was film – every waking hour.'
> George Lucas

A LOOK AT LIFE

At USC, Lucas became interested in the classic Hollywood film-makers of the 1940s and 1950s. One of the directors who impressed him most was John Ford.

Lucas' imagination was fired by the **documentaries** he watched in his classes at USC. He was especially intrigued by the way the camera was used to capture images. When the student film-makers were each given one minute (10 metres) of film to see how a camera worked, most of the other students did just that. They just moved the camera up and down to see what happened. Some filmed animated drawings or moved objects in **stop-motion** photography, as Lucas had done when he was twelve. But Lucas made a movie.

IN THE JOHN FORD TRADITION OF GREATNESS.   JOHN FORD AND MERIAN C. COOPER Present
JOHN WAYNE - JOANNE DRU - JOHN AGAR - BEN JOHNSON - HARRY CAREY, JR.
IN   "SHE WORE A YELLOW RIBBON"
with VICTOR McLAGLEN · MILDRED NATWICK · GEORGE O'BRIEN · ARTHUR SHIELDS   Colour by TECHNICOLOR
Story by JAMES WARNER BELLAH   DIRECTED BY JOHN FORD   Produced by ARGOSY PICTURES CORPORATION
Screen Play by FRANK NUGENT and LAURENCE STALLINGS   Distributed by RKO RADIO PICTURES.

> 'Learning to make films is very easy. Learning what to make films about is very hard.'
> George Lucas

Lucas took photographs from *Life* magazines: pictures of girls, politicians, babies, and other images that revealed what the United States was like in 1964. He zoomed in on some of the photos, **panned** across others, and experimented with the quick **cuts** that have come to characterize most of his films. He also added a soundtrack. He called his film *A Look at Life*. His professor was so impressed that he encouraged Lucas to submit his movie to several student film festivals. It won numerous awards.

Lucas shot to the top of the class. He also cemented friendships with many of the other film students. Lucas helped to record sound, **edit**, or whatever else was needed on the other students' projects, and they did the same for him.

When Lucas was nearing the completion of his course, his father attended the screening of one of his student films. George Snr was impressed by what he saw and by the way the audience reacted to it. He gave his son extra money, which Lucas used to make further films.

MAKING THE TRANSITION

After graduation, Lucas knew he might be drafted to serve in the armed forces in Vietnam, where the United States was involved in a war. He decided to **enlist** instead. That way he thought he might be given a better assignment. But the armed forces turned him down because he was **diabetic**.

Lucas decided to return to USC. It was too late to enrol as a graduate student that year, but the school gave him a job teaching evening classes. He also found work on a **documentary** about President Lyndon Johnson.

Lucas with Marcia Griffin.

While working on the documentary, Lucas met a film editor named Marcia Griffin. She had also grown up in Modesto. At first there was competition between them. He was an intellectual from the university; she was a professional editor working in the film industry. He was shy and something of a nerd. She was outgoing and quite pretty. But eventually they began dating and fell in love. They married in 1969.

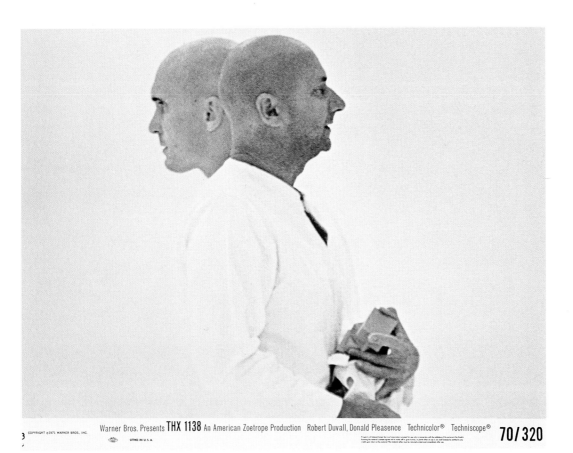

Warner Bros. Presents THX 1138 An American Zoetrope Production   Robert Duvall, Donald Pleasence   Technicolor® Techniscope®   **70/320**

Robert Duvall and Donald Pleasence in the final film version of *THX 1138*. In the meantime, Lucas worked on a master's degree at USC. His graduate project, *THX 1138 4EB*, was a fifteen-minute film telling the story of a future, underground world in which everyone was always under **surveillance**. THX (pronounced Thex) is the name of the main character, who attempts to escape from this world. The film won first prize in the drama category at the National Student Film Festival and helped Lucas win the Samuel Warner Scholarship. This consisted of six months at the Warner Bros film studio with a salary of $80 a week.

To Feature Films

When Lucas arrived at Warner Bros in June 1967, the only film in production was *Finian's Rainbow*, a musical starring Fred Astaire and Petula Clark. Its director – Francis Ford Coppola – was already a legend. Five years older than Lucas and also university educated, Coppola had made it to Hollywood on the strength of his talent and his self-confidence. Some thought he had sold his artistic **integrity** by agreeing to work within the commercial system (he had started out making low-budget films), but many were impressed that this young man had forced Hollywood to notice him.

The first meeting between Coppola and Lucas was uneventful. Coppola barely noticed the short, skinny kid dressed in jeans and a T-shirt. Lucas was one of the people who thought Coppola had sold out, and wasn't sure what he could learn from him. But the two found they shared the same passion for

Francis Ford Coppola at work in his studio in 1970.

> 'My success wasn't based on how I could push down everyone around me. My success was based on how much I could push everyone up. And eventually their success was the same way. And in the process they pushed me up, and I pushed them up, and we kept doing that, and we still do that.'
>
> George Lucas

extending the boundaries of film-making, and they became friends. So, when Coppola signed a three-picture deal with the studio, he made sure there was a place on the crew for Lucas.

THE MAVERICKS

Lucas and Coppola dreamed of starting their own film production company outside of Hollywood. They wanted their company to be like film school, making low-budget, experimental films that explored new possibilities in cinema. But Coppola also wanted to take advantage of his Hollywood connections.

He approached Warner Bros, asking them to finance the start-up for the company. He told the studio that their first film would be another version of *THX 1138 4EB*, directed by Lucas. Though Lucas hated writing, Coppola persuaded him to produce a full-length **screenplay** for it. After that, Coppola promised, there would be six more films, none of them costing more than a million dollars, a small sum for a movie, even in those days. Warners agreed to lend him the money on one condition: that if *THX 1138 4EB* was a flop, Coppola would have to pay them back every cent.

AMERICAN ZOETROPE

The former
American
Zoetrope building
in San Francisco.

Coppola and Lucas called their company American Zoetrope (they got the name from a device called a zoetrope, which rotates and creates seemingly moving pictures) and set up shop in San Francisco.

But there were problems right from the start. There was never enough money, and the young film-makers they attracted were all mostly interested in looking out for themselves.

THX 1138 REVISITED

Lucas threw himself into the job of directing *THX 1138* (he agreed to shorten the title). But the resulting picture was confusing to the production people at Warners. They withdrew their financial support from American Zoetrope and insisted on having one of their people **edit** the film. This infuriated Lucas, who held a grudge against Warners for many years after. When the film was finally released, it was shown primarily on the **art-house** and student circuits, instead of in mainstream cinemas. It didn't receive much attention or make much money, but some critics were impressed, and the Los Angeles PBS station made an hour-long documentary about Lucas. When the

The former American Zoetrope building in San Francisco.

> 'The cuts [by the studio on THX 1138] didn't make the movie any better; they had absolutely no effect on the movie at all. It was a very personal kind of film, and I didn't think they had the right to come in and just **arbitrarily** chop it up at their own whim.'
>
> George Lucas

prestigious Cannes Film Festival asked to include *THX 1138* in its programme, Lucas received even more attention – and the chance to pitch another idea he had: a rock and roll movie about **cruising**.

Lucas' wife, Marcia, and Coppola had both admired the technical **expertise** of *THX 1138*, but they thought it somewhat cold and humourless. Coppola, in particular, encouraged Lucas to write something warmer and more human. Although he had an idea for a science fiction movie, Lucas decided to develop an idea from his own life. He called it *American Graffiti*. And, as American Zoetrope was sinking into bankruptcy and anarchy, Lucas looked to the Hollywood studios for financial backing.

The men with beards

One of the ways in which Francis Ford Coppola influenced George Lucas had nothing whatsoever to do with film. Coppola sports a big, bushy beard. When Lucas first began working with him, Coppola advised him that 'people respect a bearded man more'. Lucas subsequently grew a beard, and has kept it to this day.

AMERICAN GRAFFITI

The president of United Artists, David Picker, was impressed by Lucas and by the outline of *American Graffiti*. He agreed to give Lucas an advance of $10,000 for a full **screenplay**. Lucas was thrilled. But when the screenplay was finished, Picker changed his mind. He felt that there wasn't a market for 'youth films' and decided not to continue the project. It wasn't in Lucas' character to quit. He took the screenplay to every major studio in Hollywood. Finally Universal agreed to take it – if Coppola would agree to **produce** it.

A scene from American Graffiti.

Despite the troubles at American Zoetrope, Coppola had scored huge personal successes with his screenplay for *Patton – Lust for Glory* and his direction of *The Godfather.* Lucas didn't like having to go cap in hand to him. But he swallowed his pride and approached Coppola who agreed to work with him on the project.

A good idea

Lucas worked with film editor, Walter Murch, on the **soundtrack** for *American Graffiti*. Murch asked Lucas for some film, which was identified as R2, D2 (Reel 2, Dialogue 2). Lucas liked the way that sounded and made a note of it. He thought it might make a good name for a character someday – maybe a cute robot.

American Graffiti tells the story of four young men: Curt, an introvert who has won a scholarship to college; Steve, the class president; Terry, the gauche nerd; and John Milner, the king of the **drag racers**. The action of the film takes place on a single night, from dusk to dawn, as each of these young men reaches a turning point in his life. The plot cuts quickly from one storyline to the next, but the whole is held together by the rock and roll music soundtrack, recorded as if playing on the radios of the **cruising** cars. *American Graffiti* is both a wonderfully **nostalgic** look at life in the 1950s and early 1960s and a sensitive tale about growing up. It features many young actors who would later become stars: Harrison Ford, Ron Howard, Richard Dreyfuss, Charles Martin Smith, Paul Le Mat, Cindy Williams, Candy Clark, Mackenzie Phillips and Suzanne Somers. Lucas shot the film in just twenty-eight days with a total budget of $750,000.

SUCCESS

Lucas was completely unprepared for the reaction to *American Graffiti*. When the executives at Universal previewed it, they didn't like it. As with *THX 1138*, they insisted on Lucas turning the film over to their editor (who made about 2 ½ minutes of cuts – which Lucas was eventually able to restore). The executives even considered not releasing it. But when two other studios approached them to buy the film and release it themselves, Universal decided to send it out.

> 'After I did *American Graffiti*, and it was successful, it was a big moment for me... I knew at that point, I'd made it. There wasn't anything in my life that was going to stop me from making movies.'
>
> George Lucas

American Graffiti premiered on 1 August 1973. Lucas was so nervous that he and Marcia decided to skip the premiere and take a long overdue vacation in Hawaii. But the critics and the audiences loved it. The *Los Angeles Times* called it 'one of the most important films of the year'. It was nominated for five Oscars, eventually went on to make more than $200 million, and now ranks seventy-seventh in the American Film Institute's list of the 100 best movies ever made.

Lucas was stunned and then overjoyed. This unexpected success meant freedom. He now had the financial resources and the clout to make movies his way. He decided to pursue another of his movie ideas, a little science fiction thing. It wouldn't be a deeply significant, intellectual movie. What he had in mind was a film based on a comic book approach — with lots of action and swashbuckling fun.

American Graffiti, one of the 100 best movies ever made.

Star Wars

Even before the success of *American Graffiti*, Twentieth Century Fox had signed a preliminary agreement with Lucas for *The Star Wars*, as it was then called. Now he was Hollywood's hottest new director and they were willing to commit to the new project and increase the budget. They were surprised that Lucas didn't try to increase the salary he would receive for directing. For Lucas, it was more important to have control over the film and any sequels. Lucas also asked for most of the rights to *Star Wars* **merchandise**. As no one had ever made much money selling film-related merchandise, Fox didn't hesitate to agree to that.

Myths and motifs

It took Lucas about two years to write the **screenplay**. As he never enjoyed writing, this was agonizingly hard work. Early drafts featured a main character called Anakin Starkiller, a Jedi-Bendu knight. There was an older warrior called General Skywalker and a green-skinned alien named Han Solo. As he wrote and rewrote, Lucas studied science fiction novels and films and researched **mythology**. He was particularly struck by the ideas of Joseph Campbell, who suggested that each generation retells the same stories. The ideas and themes stay the same, only the places and names change. There was just one problem with the screenplay that Lucas finally produced. It was far too long. He would have to film just a third of it, saving the remainder for sequels.

'With *Star Wars*, I consciously set about to recreate myths and the classic mythological **motifs**. I wanted to use those motifs to deal with issues that exist today. The more research I did, the more I realized that the issues are the same ones that existed 3,000 years ago. That we haven't come very far emotionally.'

George Lucas

Putting it all together

Lucas worked hard assembling a cast and choosing filming locations. He finally chose Mark Hamill to play Luke Skywalker, Harrison Ford for Han Solo,

Carrie Fisher for Princess Leia and Alec Guinness for Obi-Wan Kenobi. Dave Prowse would play Darth Vader (although James Earl Jones provided his voice), Peter Mayhew was Chewbacca, Anthony Daniels was C-3PO, and Kenny Baker played R2-D2. To save money, Lucas planned to shoot in a studio outside London, as it was cheaper to make a film in the UK than in Hollywood. The desert scenes would be shot in Tunisia.

Sir Alec Guinness, who played Obi-Wan Kenobi in Star Wars.

Lucas believed the hardest part of the project would be obtaining the special effects he wanted. From the very beginning, Lucas knew he wanted to present spectacular special effects, unlike any that had ever been done before. But the technology for what he wanted to do simply didn't exist in 1975.

'*Star Wars* was a **seminal** moment when the entire industry was instantly changed. For me, it's when the world recognized the value of childhood.'
Steven Spielberg

INDUSTRIAL LIGHT AND MAGIC

Lucas formed a special company – the Industrial Light and Magic Company (ILM) – to produce the special effects he wanted. He hired John Dykstra, a special-effects technician, to head it. Dykstra had invented a camera that moved on a track while filming a model. Its movement could be repeated over and over again, exactly the same every time. Prior to this, the camera remained motionless while the model moved. By filming a model spaceship with the new camera, and using the same technique to film a second one, and then by **superimposing** one sequence over the other, Dykstra could create a **dogfight** in space. Lucas was sure that Dykstra could come up with equally ingenious ways of producing the other effects he wanted.

Money was extremely tight. Lucas cut corners wherever he could. For the finale, in which Princess Leia presents Luke

Star Wars co-stars Carrie Fisher and Mark Hamill.

Skywalker and Han Solo with medals, Lucas used cardboard cutouts for most of the background figures because he couldn't afford to hire enough extras to represent the rebel soldiers.

The production was plagued with problems: sets were not finished on time, unexpected rain held up filming, and the heat was nearly unendurable for the actors in costume. The principal characters found many of their lines were too complicated, and they argued about how to speak them. The crew went weeks over schedule filming the dialogue scenes. Then Lucas returned to Los Angeles to find that ILM had finished only three of the four hundred special effects he needed. In Hollywood it was rumoured that *Star Wars* was going to be a complete flop. Lucas ended up in hospital suffering from exhaustion. He vowed that if he ever finished this film, he'd never direct again.

"The whole Lucas emphasis is on special effects, on loading the film with optical tricks that can be created only in movies, [and this] opens the audience's mind… to the connections between a seemingly simple tale and the richer realms of myth.'

Film critic Richard Schickel

Getting it finished

Lucas did get it finished, but he was frustrated that he'd only been able to get part of what he'd pictured in his mind on to film. The one thing that turned out better than Lucas had imagined it would was the brilliant musical score by John Williams.

Nobody believed that the film would be a hit. It opened in only 32 cinemas across the United States, because only 32 cinemas agreed to book it.

Public reaction

Lucas vividly remembers the day *Star Wars* opened on 25 May 1977. When he and Marcia went out to dinner that evening, they noticed a line that snaked round the **block** at the local cinema. When they checked to see what the crowd was waiting for,

'*Star Wars* is made up of many themes. It's not just one little simple **parable**. One is our relationship to machines, which are fearful, but also **benign**. Then there is the lesson of friendship and **symbiotic** relationships, of your obligations to your fellow man, to other people that are around you. This is a world where evil has run amuck. But you have control over your destiny, and you have many paths to walk down, and you can choose which destiny is going to be yours.'

George Lucas

Lucas couldn't believe it. The people were waiting to see *Star Wars!* The same thing happened everywhere that *Star Wars* played. By the end of the summer, the film would still be in the cinemas – showing on more than 800 screens.

An Academy Award statuette, also known as an 'Oscar'.

Star Wars was nominated for ten Academy Awards, including Best Picture and Best Director, but it won only technical awards: for Art Direction, Sound, Original Score, **Editing**, and Visual Effects. The Hollywood insiders were still erecting barriers against upstart newcomers. Twenty years later, the American Film Institute finally acknowledged what George Lucas had achieved by ranking *Stars Wars* at number 15 on its list of the 100 best movies ever made.

But the public couldn't get enough of the movie. People returned to the cinemas to see it over and over again. It has made more than $460,000,000 at the box office, which means that it is currently the second highest grossing movie of all time. Only *Titanic* has grossed more. And when the 1977 ticket prices are adjusted to the 1997 level, *Star Wars* comes out on top.

To Infinity, and Beyond

The incredible success of *Star Wars* made George Lucas a multi-millionaire. This enabled him to become completely independent of Hollywood. He could finance any picture he wanted to make. Any deal he might make with a Hollywood studio would be entirely on his own terms.

Lucas was firm in his decision not to direct again. He found it too exhausting, and he didn't like working with actors. But that didn't mean he'd have to stop making films. By providing the story idea and serving as the executive **producer**, he could control a major part of the film-making process.

Steven Spielberg (left) and George Lucas leave their handprints in cement at Hollywood's Chinese Theatre.

He joined forces with his friend and fellow director, Steven Spielberg. They decided to make a picture together based on another 'little idea' of Lucas'. It was a story about this adventurous guy called Indiana Jones who wore a felt hat and carried a whip. Their film became *Raiders of the Lost Ark*, and would rank sixtieth on the American Film Institute's list of the 100 best films ever made.

Over the next few years, Lucas served as executive producer on a number of pictures. These included the two *Stars Wars* sequels – *The Empire Strikes Back* and *Return of the Jedi* – and two sequels to *Raiders of the Lost Ark* – *Indiana Jones and the Temple of Doom* and *Indiana Jones and the Last Crusade*. These would become four of the most successful and popular movies ever made. There were a few flops too, however, including *More American Graffiti* and *Howard the Duck*, but Lucas' name alone was enough to launch just about any picture. Unfortunately, his personal life did not parallel this success.

PUBLIC SUCCESS, PERSONAL DIFFICULTIES

Lucas and his wife learned they could not have children. In 1981 they adopted a baby girl whom they named Amanda. Lucas adored her, but had little time to spend with her or his wife. In 1982, George and Marcia decided to divorce. Many feel that the darker tone of *Indiana Jones and the Temple of Doom* was the result of Lucas' gloom after his divorce. He threw himself into his work.

Eventually Lucas adopted two more children, another girl and a boy, and by the early 1990s had become less and less involved with films. It took a new challenge to pull him back into that world.

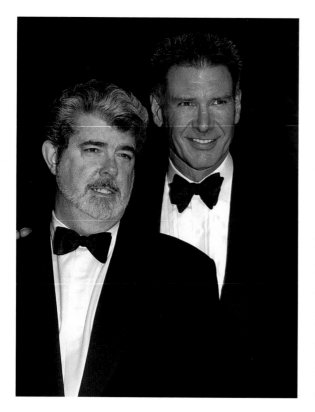

Lucas with actor Harrison Ford, who played Indiana Jones.

Lucas had always been interested in education. But the only things to grab his attention at school were the films that had been shown in class. From these he decided that there were more exciting ways to convey information to kids than being lectured at by a teacher.

> 'One of the basic **motifs** in fairy tales is that you find the poor and unfortunate along the side of the road, and when they beg for help, if you give it to them, you end up succeeding. If you don't give it to them, you end up being turned into a frog or something.'
>
> George Lucas

In 1991 he started the George Lucas Educational Foundation. Its aim was to improve the quality of public education by producing classroom materials that challenge students and engage them in learning. To this end, Lucas decided to make a TV series about the young Indiana Jones. In it, Indiana would have adventures all over the world, and meet people who were important in history.

Lucas approached the ABC television network. They liked the idea and launched *The Young Indiana Jones Chronicles*. The series began with a two-hour 'movie of the week', followed by weekly one-hour episodes. Lucas was executive producer. Though some critics praised it, the series never really caught on. Viewers who expected non-stop action found its history lessons too slow.

However, it sparked Lucas' interest in directing again. Technological advances had made that job easier. And when a new *Star Wars* book, *Heir to the Empire*, surprised everyone by topping the *New York Times* bestseller list, Lucas began thinking about doing a new *Star Wars* movie.

The Special Edition

First Lucas used the new technology to create special editions of the original three movies. With computer animation, he was able to add some of the details he hadn't had enough money to create the first time, such as more aliens and more spaceships.

The special edition pulled in more than $36 million at the box office the first weekend after it was released. This overwhelming reaction convinced Lucas that the time was right to do the first three chapters of the *Star Wars* saga. These tell the story of how Anakin Skywalker became Darth Vader, the villain of *Star Wars*. And, for the first time in almost twenty years, Lucas would write the script and direct.

The Phantom Menace

The public reaction to *The Phantom Menace* was mixed. Though it took more than $100 million at the box office in the first five days after its release,

A fan dressed in a Darth Maul outfit at the premiere of *Star Wars: The Phantom Menace* in London.

Optical illusion

For the Boonta Eve pod race in *The Phantom Menace*, the technicians built a 13m by 13m model of the stadium. But when it came time to film, there was a problem. How could they make it look as if the stadium was filled with 350,000 spectators? After a great deal of thought and experimentation, they found a unique solution. They painted cotton swabs different colours and placed them in a wire mesh screen. Then they blew air on them to create the illusion of the restless movement of a crowd. On screen, it looks just like a crowd of fans at a football game.

audience attendance began to fall off soon after. The special effects are spectacular – it is nearly impossible to tell what is real and what is computer-generated. The backgrounds contain all the rich details Lucas always wanted in his films. This is a fantasy world that the audience can believe is real. And the action sequences, such as the pod race, are exciting. But the characters seem flat and uninteresting. The first *Star Wars* appealed to young and old, rich and poor, male and female. *The Phantom Menace* was designed for twelve-year-old boys – and they loved it.

Lucas was content that he'd reached his target audience and done what he'd set out to do. He began to work on his plans for Chapter 2. And he would do it his way.

LUCAS' LEGACY

In *The Empire Strikes Back*, Yoda cautions Luke Skywalker: 'Judge me not by my size'. This could be George Lucas speaking instead. Although he is only 1.75 metres tall, many have said that he's the most powerful man in the film industry. And no one can doubt the influence and the importance of his films. When asked how he's managed to do all the things he's done, Lucas invariably responds, 'I just did it'. He didn't stand around wishing that something would happen. He worked hard to make it happen. Sometimes he failed, but he never let that discourage him.

'If it [*Star Wars*] were just an adrenaline-rush movie, it wouldn't be here 20 years later. There are other things going on that are complicated and psychologically satisfying.'

George Lucas

A Star Wars fan clutches a precious bunch of cinema tickets.

> 'They [the *Star Wars* films] address our hunger for **mythology**, but they don't meet it. The way these films simplistically frame the fight between good and evil contributes to our inability to live with moral complexity.'
> Lewis Hyde, professor of art and politics at Kenyon College, Gambier, Ohio, USA

Lucas' very first film was of a special effect: plates that stacked and unstacked themselves. In his films he has turned special effects into an advanced art form. The worlds he creates and the excitement he generates are truly stupendous. And yet they also reveal what many feel to be his major weakness: that he is more interested in machines than in people.

Lucas has been credited with bringing back the 'feel-good' film as well as the action adventure, and many believe that to be a good thing. They think it is an advantage to encourage people to be optimistic. Others, however, think that this is too simple a way of looking at life. They want films to encourage people to think more deeply.

Star Wars revisited

For the twentieth anniversary reissue of the *Star Wars* trilogy, Lucas was able to go back and clean up the special effects, adding lots of digital backgrounds and computer-generated creatures. He also included some additional details, such as a new scene between Han Solo and Jabba the Hut.

Skywalker ranch

Lucas has taken millions of dollars earned from his movies and invested them in something he hopes will be part of his legacy: the Skywalker Ranch. This 1,000-hectare ranch outside San Francisco includes a mansion, which contains Lucas' private office, stables, guest houses, a two-storey library, a huge sound studio, various post-production facilities, the Lucas Archives, an artificial lake and extensive wooded grounds. When Lucas first started it, in 1978, he hoped to house a film community there like the one that he and Francis Coppola had tried to create with American Zoetrope. He envisaged lots of young film-makers experimenting with new ideas, away from the corruption of Hollywood. The more successful he became, however, the fewer people he was willing to admit to the ranch. Today it is a state-of-the-art movie production facility. But most of the time, only well-established film people can afford to use it.

'I'm very conscious of the environments and I try to have at least three environments in a movie, and I try to have them as different as possible. Then, from movie to movie, I try to have the environments as different as possible. There's a whole colour and environment **motif** that goes through, and the good guys are all earth colours and the bad guys are all colourless.'

George Lucas

Some of the profits that helped to build Skywalker Ranch came from Lucas' film-**merchandising** business. Today it is usual for action figures, hats, mugs, lunch boxes and so on to be sold in connection with the release of a film; these various items of merchandise usually include pictures of the film's characters on them. But before *Star Wars* such items were rare. In fact, many people blame the entire film–merchandising business on *Star Wars*. Few people think that merchandising is a good thing. And some films have been accused of being nothing more than commercials for new toys.

'What I wanted to build was a work environment that is a model of the way I think creative people should be allowed to work.'

George Lucas talking about the Skywalker Ranch

Hero or Villain?

So is George Lucas a creative genius whose numerous **innovations** have **enhanced** the film-making process? Or is he the man whose influence made Hollywood focus more on special effects and less on story-line? Both these claims have been made, but perhaps the truth lies somewhere in between. No one can deny that Lucas has changed the way in which films are made. In films such as *Star Wars*, the stories he tells are simple ones. But the techniques he uses to present those stories on the screen are definitely not simple.

Lucas **lavishes** attention on the images he offers the audience. In *Star Wars*, picture the contrast between the stark blacks and whites of the Imperial fleet and the soft earth tones of Yoda's home planet. Study the outlandish creatures that populate the worlds into which he guides his viewers – creatures such as Jabba the Hut, C-3PO or Chewbacca. The visual details sometimes pass by in seconds, but they help to create an entire fantasy universe.

A technological wizard

Lucas' inventiveness is not limited to the content of his films. He has also pioneered spectacular special effects and digital sound. Before *Star Wars*, special effects were almost dead in Hollywood. The failure of big-screen epics had caused most motion picture studios to close down their special effects divisions. Instead, they concentrated on small, intimate films set in the real world. But Lucas envisioned a film that spanned the galaxy. He wanted light-sabre duels, thrilling spaceship **dogfights**, and spectacular explosions.

Some people in the film business told him nobody wanted to see that stuff, and that the technology didn't exist to make the sort of film he dreamed about anyway. But he enlisted the help of others who shared his vision. Together they developed the equipment and techniques that could create the kind of effects Lucas wanted. His special effects company, Industrial Light and Magic, is now the foremost producer of special effects in the world.

George Lucas and Sony President Nobuyuki Idei discuss a new digital camera at a US trade fair.

Lucas' attention to detail includes not only what the audience will see, but also what it will hear. He plans the musical scores of his films **meticulously**, and labours to get each sound effect just right. On *Star Wars* his sound technician spent a year gathering and combining sounds. He wanted to achieve a perfect balance between natural and exotic. His efforts produced effects such as Chewbacca's yowl, which is a combination of bear, badger, walrus and seal. But Lucas was appalled at the way his films sounded in most cinemas. Their **antiquated** sound equipment was incapable of producing the effect he wanted. Again, he decided that if the technology didn't exist, he'd have it invented. And so his engineers developed THX Sound.

LUCAS' EFFECT ON HOLLYWOOD

Why, then, do some people say that George Lucas ruined Hollywood? The answer is simple: greed. *Star Wars* made so much money that it changed people's expectations about how much money a film should make. Almost overnight, the small, intimate film that showed just a modest profit was abandoned. Studios concentrated on making 'blockbusters'.

People also complain that Lucas contributed to the 'dumbing down' of Hollywood. They say he discarded complex plotting and character development in favour of technological wizardry and non-stop action. Lucas denies this accusation: 'The technology is not the essence of the entertainment experience. It's what you do with the technology; it's how you use that and how you manipulate it.' The same could be said of his **innovations**: it's what you do with them that determines whether they're good or bad.

Lucas with his daughter, Katie, and Steven Spielberg with his wife, Kate Capshaw, at the 1999 Golden Globe Awards.

THE FILMS OF GEORGE LUCAS

STUDENT FILMS (written, produced, and directed by Lucas):
A Look at Life (1965)
Freiheit (1965)
Herbie (1966)
1:42:08: A Man and His Car (1966)
The Emperor (1967)
THX 1138 4EB (1967)
anyone lived in a pretty (how) town (1967)
film-maker: a film diary (1968)

FEATURE FILMS:

THX 1138 (released March 1971): co-authored by George Lucas and
   Walter Murch; directed and edited by George Lucas

American Graffiti (released August 1973): co-authored by George Lucas and
   Gloria Katz and Willard Huyck; directed by George Lucas

Star Wars (released May 1977): written and directed by George Lucas;
   executive producer: George Lucas

More American Graffiti (released August 1979): executive producer:
   George Lucas

The Empire Strikes Back (released May 1980): based on a story by George
   Lucas; executive producer: George Lucas

Kagemusha (The Shadow Warrior) (released October 1980): co-executive
   producer of the international version: George Lucas (with Francis
   Ford Coppola)

Raiders of the Lost Ark (released June 1981): based on a story by George
   Lucas and Philip Kaufman; co-executive producer: George Lucas (with
   Howard Kazanjian)

Twice Upon a Time (released August 1982): executive producer:
   George Lucas

Return of the Jedi (released May 1983): based on a story by George Lucas;
   co-authored by George Lucas and Lawrence Kasdan; executive
   producer: George Lucas

Indiana Jones and the Temple of Doom (released May 1984): based on a story by George Lucas; co-executive producer: George Lucas (with Frank Marshall)

Mishima (released September 1985): co-executive producer: George Lucas (with Francis Ford Coppola)

Labyrinth (released June 1986): executive producer: George Lucas

Howard the Duck (released August 1986): executive producer: George Lucas

Captain EO (released at Disneyland, September 1986): executive producer: George Lucas

Willow (released May 1988): based on a story by George Lucas; executive producer: George Lucas

Tucker: The Man and His Dream (released August 1988): executive producer: George Lucas

The Land Before Time (released November 1988): co-executive producer: George Lucas (with Steven Spielberg)

Indiana Jones and the Last Crusade (released May 1989): based on a story by George Lucas and Menno Meyjes; co-executive producer: George Lucas (with Frank Marshall)

Radioland Murders (released October 1994): based on a story by George Lucas; executive producer: George Lucas

The Phantom Menace (released May 1999): written and directed by George Lucas; executive producer: George Lucas

TELEVISION FILMS:

The Star Wars Holiday Special (first broadcast November 1978): based on a story by George Lucas (uncredited)

The Ewok Adventure: Caravan of Courage (first broadcast November 1984): based on a story by George Lucas; executive producer: George Lucas

Ewoks: The Battle for Endor (first broadcast November 1985): based on a story by George Lucas; executive producer: George Lucas

The Young Indiana Jones Chronicles (first broadcast March 1992): based on a story by George Lucas; executive producer: George Lucas

GLOSSARY

antiquated old-fashioned, outdated

apprenticeship a period of time during which a person learns a craft or trade by working under a person already skilled in that job

arbitrarily selected or decided based on random choice or personal whim

art-house a term used to describe films made and screened outside the mainstream, commercial system

benign kind, gentle

block a group of buildings in a city

camaraderie a feeling of friendship

cruising driving around a particular area in search of entertainment

cut in film-making, to move quickly to another scene

darkroom a room in which photographs are processed

diabetic a person who suffers from diabetes, a metabolic disorder

documentary a factual film or television programme

dogfights battles between two or more fighter planes or spaceships

drag race a race in which specially built cars are timed over a measured course

edit preparing a film for presentation by cutting and rearranging pieces of the film

enhance to improve

enlist to join on of the armed forces

expertise having great knowledge or skill

haemorrhaging suddenly discharging a large amount of blood

hot-rod a car with an engine modified to produce increased power

innovation a new way of doing something

integrity honesty and trustworthiness

lavish to give a large amount of something, e.g. money, attention

merchandise goods, e.g. toys and games, produced to coincide with the release of a film or television programme

Methodist a follower of the Methodist church which advocates, among other things, hard work and thrift

meticulously to do something by paying extreme attention to all the details

motifs ideas that appear over and over again, usually in literature

mythology the study of traditional stories usually dealing with legendary heroes and supernatural events

nostalgia a sentimental longing to return to or remember an idealized past

pan to move a camera across a scene

parable a short story with an ethical or religious message

produce to supervise the production of a film or television programme

screenplay the script for a film

seminal describing something like an event, a work or person who has strongly influenced later developments

soundtrack the sound portion of a film

stationer's a shop that sells paper products

stop-motion a technique for producing a special effect by stopping the camera, moving the object being filmed slightly and then starting the camera again

superimposing placing one thing over another, usually to create a single image or object

surveillance the maintenance of a careful watch over something or someone

symbiotic dependent on one another

tenacity sticking to something with stubborn determination

union a workplace association of people that looks after employees' interests

INDEX